ACTFL

Performance Descriptors for Language Learners

ACTFL
Performance Descriptors for Language Learners

Language learning is complex. Many factors impact how well language learners will acquire communication skills and how quickly they will reach different ranges of performance. These factors include where one learns language, whether in an instructional setting or immersed in the language or culture; how one learns, whether through explicit instruction about the language or through authentic experiences using the language; when one learns, as the age and cognitive development of language learners impact the speed of reaching each range of performance; and finally, why one is learning a language, whether motivated by extrinsic factors such as grades and requirements or intrinsic factors such as the language learner's heritage or intended uses of the language.

Acknowledgements

The American Council on the Teaching of Foreign Languages (ACTFL) wishes to acknowledge the editors and contributing authors of this new document.
- Authors and Editors: Paul Sandrock and Elvira Swender
- Contributing authors: Maria Antonia Cowles, Cynthia Martin, and Robert Vicars

ACTFL also acknowledges the critical role of those members of the profession who reviewed these Performance Descriptors: Arnold Bleicher, Peggy Boyles, Donna Clementi, Greg Duncan, Helga Fasciano, Martin Smith, and Laura Terrill.

The ACTFL Performance Descriptors for Language Learners were built on the solid foundation provided by the original task force that produced the 1998 *ACTFL Performance Guidelines for K–12 Learners*. The members of that task force forged new ground to help educators implement the standards, providing important descriptions of how language learners demonstrate performance of the three modes of communication in instructional settings. Informed by the ACTFL Proficiency Guidelines, the 1998 task force carefully identified appropriate learning targets that impacted instruction and assessment in language classrooms across the U.S. and beyond. The new ACTFL Performance Descriptors for Language Leaners benefited from the experience of language educators implementing the original guidelines.

ACTFL acknowledges the authors of the 1998 *ACTFL Performance Guidelines for K–12 Learners*: Greg Duncan and Elvira Swender; the Section Editors: Martha Abbott, Peggy Boyles, and John Miles; and the members of the Performance Guidelines for K–12 Learners Task Force: Harriet Barnett, Karen Breiner-Sanders, Mari Haas, Eileen Lorenz, Alisha Reeves Samples, Nancy Rhodes, Kathleen Riordan, Margaret Singer.

1 About the ACTFL Performance Descriptors for Language Learners

The ACTFL Performance Descriptors for Language Learners are designed to describe language performance that is the result of explicit instruction in an instructional setting. A companion to the *ACTFL Proficiency Guidelines*, a document that describes broad, general language proficiency regardless of when, where or how language is acquired, the ACTFL Performance Descriptors for Language Learners provide more detailed and more granular information about language learners.

The *Standards for Foreign Language Learning* (1996, 1999, 2006), describe what students need to know and be able to do as they learn another language, defining the "what" of language education. The *ACTFL Performance Guidelines for K–12 Learners* (1998) first described "how well" language learners were expected to do the "what" from the content standards. The ACTFL Performance Descriptors for Language Learners are an update and revision to the 1998 *Performance Guidelines*.

The current *Standards for Foreign Language Learning* are written for K–16 and include language-specific progress indicators for elementary, secondary, and postsecondary learners. Likewise, these Performance Descriptors apply to language learners across the same span of ages and grade levels, identifying a continuum of language learning, which will prove useful in addressing articulation across all institutions.

Language learners in instructional settings from pre-kindergarten through graduate studies are in a continuous process of cognitive development that influences their ability to perform language tasks. Learning targets need to consider the age appropriateness and cognitive development of the language learners and may require varying amounts of time to achieve. The description of three ranges of performance (Novice, Intermediate, and Advanced) allows users of these Performance Descriptors to identify appropriate learning targets for language learners who begin at any age or grade level (prekindergarten, elementary school, middle school, high school, or postsecondary institutions) and whose language learning continues for varying amounts of time.

Since the original publication date of the 1998 *K–12 Guidelines*, learning environments have changed. These new Performance Descriptors reflect how language learners perform whether learning in classrooms, online, through independent project-based learning, or in blended environments.

The Performance Descriptors form a roadmap for teaching and learning, helping teachers create performance tasks targeted to the appropriate performance range, while challenging learners to also use strategies from the next higher range. In an instructional environment, the content and tasks are controlled, resulting in higher expectations of learners' performance compared to how they perform in a non-instructional environment. For example, Novice language learners use highly practiced and memorized sentences and questions within the supportive learning environment and within known contexts even though they are not yet Intermediate level language users.

These Performance Descriptors also help educators set realistic expectations at the summative assessment level. The ability to look ahead to the next range of performance allows instructors to create assessments that show what the language learner is able to do within the learner's current range as well as how well the learner is able to perform in the next higher range.

2   Comparing Performance and Proficiency

In describing language ability, the terms performance and proficiency both refer to evidence of what a language user is able to do with language. Similar strategies can be used when teaching for both performance and proficiency. Likewise, assessments of both performance and proficiency reflect purposeful communication tasks, mirroring real-world uses of language. There are also significant differences between performance and proficiency. What does each indicate?

Performance

Performance is the ability to use language that has been learned and practiced in an instructional setting. Coached by an instructor, whether in a classroom or online, or guided by instructional materials, performance refers to language ability that has been practiced and is within familiar contexts and content areas. The practice and assessment of performance should reflect authentic, real world use of language, even though the language is learned and practiced in some type of learning environment. Best practices for assessment of performance suggest that assessment be conducted in the same communicative manner in which the language was learned, practiced or rehearsed. To prepare for an assessment of performance, language learners need to practice the language functions, structures, and vocabulary they will apply on the assessment tasks, rather than practicing and memorizing exactly what will be on the assessment. Educators should provide language learners with practice of a variety of tasks related to the curriculum. In this way, learners will be ready to apply these elements in the context of the new tasks they will face on the performance assessment. To help language learners transfer their language skills, instruction needs to focus on real world-like tasks with the anticipation that learners will be prepared to do the same outside the instructional setting (as in a demonstration of proficiency).

In assessing performance, a language learner is evaluated against the description of the features of the domains of a given range within those contexts and content areas that have been learned and practiced. Demonstration of performance within a specific range may provide some indication of how the language user might perform on a proficiency assessment and indeed might point toward a proficiency level, but performance is not the same as proficiency. The language a learner produces on a collective set of performances generally correlates to a proficiency level, that is, the ratings that a language learner receives on a variety of performance assessments provides evidence of how the learner will be rated on an assessment of proficiency.

Proficiency

Proficiency is the ability to use language in real world situations in a spontaneous interaction and non-rehearsed context and in a manner acceptable and appropriate to native speakers of the language. Proficiency demonstrates what a language user is able to do regardless of where, when or how the language was acquired. The demonstration is independent of how the language was learned; the context may or may not be familiar; the evaluation of proficiency is not limited to the content of a particular curriculum that has been taught and learned.

An assessment of proficiency determines if the language user provides sufficient evidence of all of the assessment criteria of a particular level according to the *ACTFL Proficiency Guidelines*. The individual must do everything expected at a level in a sustained fashion, that is, all of the time, in order to be rated at that level.

Assessing Performance vs. Assessing Proficiency: How are these assessments different?

Assessing Performance	Assessing Proficiency
• **Based on Instruction:** Describes what the language learner can demonstrate based on what was learned	• **Independent of specific instruction or curriculum:** Describes what the language user can do regardless of where, when or how the language was acquired
• **Practiced:** Tasks are derived from the language functions and vocabulary that learners have practiced or rehearsed but which are applied to other tasks within familiar contexts	• **Spontaneous:** Tasks are non-rehearsed situations
• **Familiar Content and Context:** Content based on what was learned, practiced, or rehearsed; all within a context similar but not identical to how learned	• **Broad Content and Context:** Context and content are those that are appropriate for the given level
• **Demonstrated performance:** To be evaluated within a range, must be able to demonstrate the features of the domains of a given range in those contexts and content areas that have been learned and practiced.	• **Sustained performance across all the tasks and contexts for the level:** To be at a level, must demonstrate consistent patterns of all the criteria for a given level, all of the time

3 How the Performance Descriptors Are Organized

The ACTFL Performance Descriptors for Language Learners describe how language learners use language across three ranges of performance (Novice, Intermediate, and Advanced), in three modes of communication (interpersonal, interpretive, and presentational), and according to certain language features.

According to Ranges of Performance

Each range is defined by a set of features for the range explaining what the language learner is able to do, in what contexts and content areas, how much and what kind of language the learner is able to produce or understand, the expectations of accuracy, and what strategies the language learner uses to communicate. The three ranges take into consideration that the learning environment is controlled and articulated, allowing learners to demonstrate greater control of certain features of a level when these have been practiced in familiar contexts.

A language learner who demonstrates the overall features for a given range, whether most of the time or all of the time, would be considered to be in that range of performance. In a proficiency context, a language user who meets the criteria for the Intermediate level, but is not able to do so for some content areas or tasks all of the time in spontaneous, unrehearsed, language use would be rated Novice High. In the Performance Descriptors, the same profile would place the learner as entering into the Intermediate range because most of the time, and for those tasks and content areas that have been learned and practiced, the performance is in the Intermediate range as defined by the performance domains (see page 8). Likewise, the language learner who meets the criteria for the Advanced range most of the time (and who would be rated Intermediate-High on a proficiency scale) would be considered to be entering into the Advanced range of performance. The Superior range of performance is not addressed in these Performance Descriptors because within and beyond the Advanced range, performance and proficiency tend to merge. Once students sustain language ability beyond the Advanced range, where contexts and content areas are defined in general and broad terms, the *ACTFL Proficiency Guidelines* should be used to describe language abilities.

Over time and with practice, learner's performance gradually takes on the characteristics of the next higher range of performance.

Novice Range	Intermediate Range	Advanced Range

According to Modes of Communication

The three modes of communication provide the organizing principle for describing language performance across three ranges of performance: Novice, Intermediate, and Advanced. The *ACTFL Proficiency Guidelines* were developed for purposes of assessment across four skills (listening, speaking, reading, and writing) and originated prior to the Standards. The 2012 revision of the *Proficiency Guidelines* considers how each skill is used, for example, describing both interpersonal and presentational aspects of speaking. The Performance Descriptors embrace the communicative purpose behind the three modes of communication, describing how a language learner performs to achieve each communicative purpose: interpersonal, interpretive, and presentational. The language functions are appropriately matched to the mode of communication (e.g., in the Intermediate range, a hallmark function for Interpersonal is the ability to ask, understand, and answer questions; for Interpretive, a key function is to comprehend main ideas and identify some supporting details; for Presentational, an essential function is the ability to present information by creating with language). One can also observe significant differences in the communication strategies that language learners use in each of the modes.

Three Modes of Communication

Interpersonal	Interpretive	Presentational
Active negotiation of meaning among individuals	Interpretation of what the author, speaker, or producer wants the receiver of the message to understand	Creation of messages to inform, explain, persuade, or narrate
Participants observe and monitor one another to see how their meanings and intentions are being communicated	One-way communication with no recourse to the active negotiation of meaning with the writer, speaker, or producer	One-way communication intended to facilitate interpretation by members of the other culture where no direct opportunity for the active negotiation of meaning between members of the two cultures exists
Adjustments and clarifications are made accordingly	Interpretation differs from comprehension and translation in that interpretation implies the ability to read (or listen or view) "between the lines," including understanding from within the cultural mindset or perspective	To ensure the intended audience is successful in its interpretation, the "presenter" needs knowledge of the audience's language and culture
Speaking and listening (conversation); reading and writing (text messages or via social media)	Reading (websites, stories, articles), listening (speeches, messages, songs), or viewing (video clips) of authentic materials	Writing (messages, articles, reports), speaking (telling a story, giving a speech, describing a poster), or visually representing (video or PowerPoint)

According to Language Domains

An overarching description of the range highlights the key points that distinguish the performance of Novice, Intermediate, and Advanced language learners. The description outlines the range of performance for the given mode of communication: interpersonal, interpretive, or presentational.

The first three domains describe the parameters for the language learner's performance in each range:

What are the parameters for the language learner's performance?

Domain	Examples	What it describes
Functions	• Ask formulaic questions • Initiate, maintain, and end a conversation • Create with language • Narrate and describe • Make inferences	Functions are the global tasks the learner can perform in the language
Contexts and Content	• Oneself • One's immediate environment • General interest • Work-related	Contexts are situations within which the learner can function; Content is the topics which the learner can understand and discuss
Text Type	• Words • Phrases • Sentences • Questions • Strings of sentences • Connected sentences • Paragraphs	Text type controlled by the learner is that which the learner is able to understand and produce in order to perform the functions of the level

The next four domains describe how well the language learner demonstrates performance of the functions for the level, within the corresponding contexts and content for the level, using the text type(s) appropriate for that level. An overarching description of these four domains of performance is comprehension and comprehensibility. These four categories answer the question "How and how well is the language learner able to be understood and to understand?"

How and how well is the language learner able to be understood and to understand?

Domain	What it answers	What it describes
Language Control	How accurate is the language learner's language?	Describes the level of control the learner has over certain language features or strategies to produce or understand language
Vocabulary	How extensive and applicable is the language learner's vocabulary?	Describes the parameters of vocabulary used to produce or understand language
Communication Strategies	How does the language learner maintain communication and make meaning?	Describes the strategies used to negotiate meaning, to understand text and messages, and to express oneself
Cultural Awareness	How is the language learner's cultural knowledge reflected in language use?	Describes the cultural products, practices, or perspectives the language learner may employ to communicate more successfully in the cultural setting

4 How To Use the Performance Descriptors To Inform Classroom Instruction and Assessment

The Performance Descriptors provide guidance for instruction. They match the progression of language learning and inform the planning and sequencing of instruction. These descriptions of performance provide an outline to identify instructional outcomes. Educators use these performance outcomes as the starting point for planning instruction, in a backward design model. With a clear focus on what performance should look like at the end of a unit, instructional and practice activities drive toward those outcomes. This outline describes the range of performance broadly enough for instructors to adapt to language learners of all ages; the instructors then guide language learning by considering the cognitive and developmental appropriateness of their learning activities, their multiple ways to practice language skills, and their variety of assessments.

In instruction, activities are scaffolded, that is supported by the instructor by pre-teaching critical elements such as key vocabulary or a new structure or practice of a language function. With such support, language learners are helped to perform at the next range by learning to use language at that next level. As the support is removed, language learners gradually over time become able to demonstrate that performance on their own. In this way, language learners begin to show characteristics of the next range as they approach the top end of their current performance range.

Instruction targets the next level and assessment provides language learners with the opportunity to show what they can do – with or without assistance in the form of a controlled context or content, practice and preparation, or rephrasing and paraphrasing to increase comprehension. Instructors need to target instruction across two ranges, broadening learners' performance at their current range and working to develop some abilities at the next higher range. Novice students, for example, need instruction and practice to improve their performance within the Novice level while simultaneously targeting the functions and contexts of the Intermediate range. Novice students need to experience Intermediate language in controlled and supported activities in order to gradually acquire the knowledge and strategies they will need in order to become confident and independent users of language in the Intermediate range. Instructors should consider recycling content and contexts at the next higher level of functions, providing multiple opportunities for learners to expand into the next performance range, developing stronger language control, vocabulary, communication strategies, and cultural awareness.

Unique Applications to Classical Languages

The Performance Descriptors are also intended to be applied to the classical languages (Latin and Greek). While often falsely assumed that students of Latin and classical Greek spend all of their instructional time reading and translating, these Performance Descriptors provide a further context for a more comprehensive view of the instructional components to be found in such classes. The importance of the three modes of communication as an applicable principle to the learning of the classical languages is evident in the communication standards from the *Standards for Classical Languages*:

- Students read, understand and interpret Latin or Greek
- Students use orally, listen to, and write Latin or Greek as part of the language learning process.

Therefore, while reading and understanding the written messages of the ancient world is a key to communication in the study of Latin and classical Greek, the oral use of the language can also be employed to help students avoid reading or translating word-for-word as they must listen in "chunks" (several words holding the meaning or phrases) and respond spontaneously during oral communication. This practice also builds student interest and heightens understanding of and appreciation for the languages and their cultures.

Unique Applications to American Sign Language (ASL)

These Performance Descriptors are equally applicable to learners of ASL, with slight adaptations according to each mode of communication. In the interpersonal mode (signing), the visual language signed underscores the communicative importance of facial gestures and other physical clues to meaning, but learners employ basically the same communication strategies as other languages within each of the ranges of performance. The word "interpretive" needs special definition for ASL: its use to identify a mode of communication denotes receptive language or understanding, rather than the act of serving as an ASL interpreter. The "text" is either live or recorded, such as a signed message, commentary, discussion, song, or play. In the presentational mode users of ASL use the same communication strategies as other languages; however, educators may act more as coaches to assist ASL language learners with the editing and revising process in the presentational mode. Examples of ASL presentational or productive language include messages, stories, or videos. Language educators and learners need to remember that the levels of cultural awareness as described in the Performance Descriptors are as important in ASL and within the Deaf community as in other languages and cultures.

5 Time as a Critical Component for Developing Language Performance

Language educators often face undue pressure and language learners may face unreasonable expectations when unrealistic language outcomes are set for achievement in short periods of instructional time. Students require carefully planned and well-sequenced learning opportunities that provide practice in using the language in order to internalize language competencies. Time on task is a critical factor in developing performance — time spent meaningfully engaged in active skill getting and skill using in the target language by both the teacher and the learner. ACTFL's position statement sets the goal of 90% or more of target language use by the teacher and the learners both inside and outside the classroom.

The chart (on the next page) graphically illustrates the influence of time-on-task on language performance and shows what outcomes are reasonable to expect of students who begin language instruction at various points in the K–16 spectrum. The outcomes depicted in this chart reflect general approximations based on performance testing and indicate targets that are possible for all students, given standards-based programs with continuity of instruction, sufficient time on task, and learning focused on performance. While performance outcomes may vary according to the mode of communication, the expectations in this chart represent a composite of performance outcomes for interpersonal, interpretive, and presentational communication. The most common program model for language learning in this country continues to be two years of instruction at the secondary level. This model limits students to performance in the Novice range. In an increasing number of standards-based, performance-based programs with continuity and sufficient time on task (e.g., beginning in the elementary grades with at least 90 minutes of instruction per week and continuing through the secondary years), learners are reaching the Advanced range of performance. Evidence is emerging that elementary immersion programs are able to produce students that are performing well into

the Intermediate range by middle school and exiting high school in the Advanced range. These students have the potential to exit postsecondary programs approaching or at the Superior level of proficiency. Such comparisons are given with the caution that reaching each range of performance is more than simply matching hours or years of instruction. The age and cognitive development of the language learners greatly impacts language learning. The level of literacy and language performance in the learners' native language impacts their development of literacy and language performance in additional languages.

Performance Outcomes May Vary from Language to Language and from Mode to Mode

The Performance Descriptors have been written to describe realistic language performance for students at the various benchmarks along the instructional sequence, but language learners may experience different rates of progress through different modes depending on how similar their native language is to the new language. Students whose native language is English find many similarities between English and languages using a familiar alphabet such as French, German, and Spanish. These similarities aid the learner in acquisition of the new language as many of the same literacy strategies may be employed to understand written and spoken communication. When the language is similar, cognates become a very useful tool to unlock meaning and to help one remember vocabulary.

Conversely, when students encounter languages with minimal similarity to their native language, some new strategies need to be employed to understand and to be understood. American students learning Arabic, Chinese, Hindi, Japanese, Korean, Russian, Swahili, or Urdu face different language learning challenges: unfamiliar sounds, different writing systems, and new grammars. These linguistic features, which oftentimes cannot be linked to anything the language learners know in their native language, generally extend the language acquisition process. However, these challenges vary according to the mode of communication and should not change the focus on teaching for performance. With every language, some elements will be easier than others to learn. For example, when learning languages whose writing systems are unfamiliar to them, learners face the greatest challenge in interpretive reading and presentational writing, and less of a challenge with interpersonal listening and speaking.

Heritage speakers of a language learn to use their heritage language through a variety of means, often through family and community interactions, sometimes more formally in an instructional setting, The modes of communication provide educators of heritage speakers with a useful analytical tool to determine an instructional emphasis. Interpersonal communication and interpretive listening tend to be strengths for many heritage speakers. At the same time, some heritage speakers may benefit from focused support in the modes of presentational writing and interpretive reading if prior language experiences were not in an instructional setting.

How to Use This Chart

This document and chart provide guidance to educators as they reflect on their language learning curriculum and assessments. A useful approach is to compare student evidence from performance tasks and assessments to this chart in order to reflect on students' use of language. Are students performing at a level consistent with the time and effort spent? Are students "on track" to reach the expected level of performance? Alternatively, educators may read the Performance Descriptors and determine that their students do not perform at a level consistent with the time and effort spent and, therefore, seek ways of modifying their program so that students reach the targeted levels of language performance.

Language learners also benefit by understanding the Performance Descriptors and the targeted expectations shown in this chart. The ranges of performance describe a pathway for learners to keep track of progress made, to identify domains needing additional practice, and to gain a clear understanding of how to move into the next higher range of performance. By collecting and reflecting on evidence of performance, language learners are able to set their own language learning targets, motivating them to improve their performance.

Time as a critical component for developing language performance

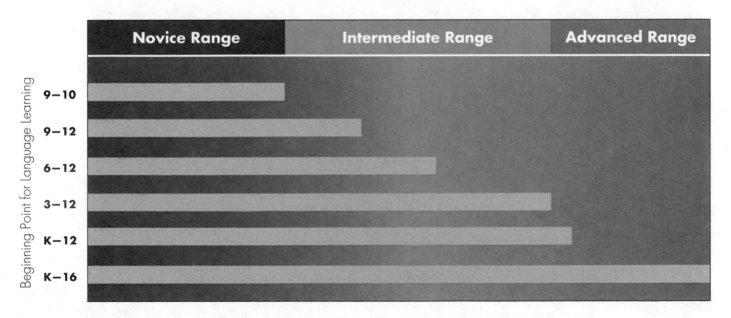

ACTFL Performance Descriptors for Language Learners | **Interpersonal**

Domains		Novice Range	Intermediate Range	Advanced Range
Domains		Expresses self in conversations on very familiar topics using a variety of words, phrases, simple sentences, and questions that have been highly practiced and memorized.	**Expresses self and participates in conversations on familiar topics using sentences and series of sentences. Handles short social interactions in everyday situations by asking and answering a variety of questions. Can communicate about self, others, and everyday life.**	**Expresses self fully to maintain conversations on familiar topics and new concrete social, academic, and work-related topics. Can communicate in paragraph-length conversation about events with detail and organization. Confidently handles situations with an unexpected complication. Shares point of view in discussions.**
Functions		Can ask highly predictable and formulaic questions and respond to such questions by listing, naming, and identifying.	Can communicate by understanding and creating personal meaning.	Can communicate with ease and confidence by understanding and producing narrations and descriptions in all major time frames and deal efficiently with a situation with an unexpected turn of events.
		May show emerging evidence of the ability to engage in simple conversation.	Can understand, ask, and answer a variety of questions.	May show emerging evidence of the ability to participate in discussions about issues beyond the concrete.
			Consistently able to initiate, maintain, and end a conversation to satisfy basic needs and/or to handle a simple transaction.	
			May show emerging evidence of the ability to communicate about more than the "here and now."	
Contexts/Content		Able to function in some personally relevant contexts on topics that relate to basic biographical information.	Able to communicate in contexts relevant to oneself and others, and one's immediate environment.	Functions fully and effectively in contexts both personal and general.
		May show emerging evidence of the ability to communicate in highly practiced contexts related to oneself and immediate environment.	May show emerging evidence of the ability to communicate in contexts of occasionally unfamiliar topics.	Content areas include topics of personal and general interest (community, national, and international events) as well as work-related topics and areas of special competence.
				May show emerging evidence of the ability to communicate in more abstract content areas.
Text Type		Understands and produces highly practiced words and phrases and an occasional sentence. Able to ask formulaic or memorized questions.	Able to understand and produce discrete sentences, strings of sentences and some connected sentences. Able to ask questions to initiate and sustain conversations.	Able to understand and produce discourse in full oral paragraphs that are organized, cohesive, and detailed. Able to ask questions to probe beyond basic details.

ACTFL Performance Descriptors for Language Learners | Interpersonal

Domains	Novice Range	Intermediate Range	Advanced Range
Language Control	Can usually comprehend highly practiced and basic messages when supported by visual or contextual clues, redundancy or restatement, and when the message contains familiar structures. Can control memorized language sufficiently to be appropriate to the context and understood by those accustomed to dealing with language learners, however at times with difficulty.	Understands straightforward language that contains mostly familiar structures. Control of language is sufficient to be understood by those accustomed to dealing with language learners.	Language control is sufficient to interact efficiently and effectively with those unaccustomed to dealing with language learners. Consistent control of basic high-frequency structures facilitates comprehension and production.
Vocabulary	Able to understand and produce a number of high frequency words, highly practiced expressions, and formulaic questions.	Communicates using high frequency and personalized vocabulary within familiar themes or topics.	Comprehends and produces a broad range of vocabulary related to school, employment, topics of personal interest, and generic vocabulary related to current events and matters or public and community interest.
Communication Strategies	May use some or all of the following strategies to maintain communication, able to: • Imitate modeled words • Use facial expressions and gestures • Repeat words • Resort to first language • Ask for repetition • Indicate lack of understanding	Uses some of the following strategies to maintain communication, but not all of the time and inconsistently, able to: • Ask questions • Ask for clarification • Self-correct or restate when not understood • Circumlocute	Uses a range of strategies to maintain communication, able to: • Request clarification • Repeat • Restate • Rephrase • Circumlocute
Cultural Awareness	May use culturally appropriate gestures and formulaic expressions in highly practiced applications. May show awareness of the most obvious cultural differences or prohibitions, but may often miss cues indicating miscommunication.	Recognizes and uses some culturally appropriate vocabulary, expressions, and gestures when participating in everyday interactions. Recognizes that differences exist in cultural behaviors and perspectives and can conform in familiar situations.	Understands and uses cultural knowledge to conform linguistically and behaviorally in many social and work-related interactions. Shows conscious awareness of significant cultural differences and attempts to adjust accordingly.

ACTFL Performance Descriptors for Language Learners | **Interpretive**

Domains	Novice Range	Intermediate Range	Advanced Range
	Understands words, phrases, and formulaic language that have been practiced and memorized to get meaning of the main idea from simple, highly-predictable oral or written texts, with strong visual support.	**Understands main ideas and some supporting details on familiar topics from a variety of texts.**	**Understands main ideas and supporting details on familiar and some new, concrete topics from a variety of more complex texts that have a clear, organized structure.**
	Comprehends meaning through recognition of key words and formulaic phrases that are highly contextualized.	Comprehends main ideas and identifies some supporting details.	Comprehends the main idea and supporting details of narrative, descriptive, and straightforward persuasive texts.
Functions	May show emerging evidence of the ability to make inferences based on background and prior knowledge.	May show emerging evidence of the ability to make inferences by identifying key details from the text.	Makes inferences and derives meaning from context and linguistic features.
Contexts/ Content	Comprehends texts with highly predictable, familiar contexts (those related to personal background, prior knowledge, or experiences).	Comprehends information related to basic personal and social needs and relevant to one's immediate environment such as self and everyday life, school, community, and particular interests.	Comprehends texts pertaining to real-world topics of general interest relevant to personal, social, work-related, community, national, and international contexts.
Text Type	Derives meaning when authentic texts (listening, reading, or viewing) are supported by visuals or when the topic is very familiar.	Comprehends simple stories, routine correspondence, short descriptive texts or other selections within familiar contexts.	Comprehends paragraph discourse such as that found in stories, straightforward literary works, personal and work-related correspondence, written reports or instructions, oral presentations (news), anecdotes, descriptive texts, and other texts dealing with topics of a concrete nature.
	Comprehends texts ranging in length from lists, to phrases, to simple sentences, often with graphically organized information.	Generally comprehends connected sentences and much paragraph-like discourse.	
		Comprehends information-rich texts with highly predictable order.	

ACTFL Performance Descriptors for Language Learners | Interpretive

Domains	Novice Range	Intermediate Range	Advanced Range
Language Control	Primarily relies on vocabulary to derive meaning from texts. May derive meaning by recognizing structural patterns that have been used in familiar and some new contexts.	Sufficient control of language (vocabulary, structures, conventions of spoken and written language, etc.) to understand fully and with ease short, non-complex texts on familiar topics; limited control of language to understand some more complex texts. May derive meaning by: • Comparing target language structures with those of the native language • Recognizing parallels in structure between new and familiar language	Sufficient control of language (vocabulary, structures, conventions of spoken and written language, etc.) to understand fully and with ease more complex and descriptive texts with connected language and cohesive devices. Derives meaning by: • Understanding sequencing, time frames, and chronology • Classifying words or concepts according to word order or grammatical use
Vocabulary	Comprehends some, but not all of the time, a limited number of words related to familiar topics, and formulaic expressions.	Comprehends high frequency vocabulary related to everyday topics and high frequency idiomatic expressions.	Comprehends generic and some specific vocabulary and structures, specialized and precise vocabulary on topics related to one's experience, and an expanding number of idiomatic expressions.
Communication Strategies	May use some or all of the following strategies to comprehend texts, able to: • Skim and scan • Rely on visual support and background knowledge • Predict meaning based on context, prior knowledge, and/or experience For alphabetic languages: • Reply on recognition of cognates • May recognize word family roots, prefixes and suffixes	May use some or all of the following strategies to comprehend texts, able to: • Skim and scan • Use visual support and background knowledge • Predict meaning based on context, prior knowledge, and/or experience • Use context clues • Recognize word family roots, prefixes and suffixes For non-alphabetic languages: • Recognize radicals	Comprehends fully the intent of the message adapting strategies for one's own purposes; uses some or all of the following strategies, able to: • Skim and scan • Use visual support and background knowledge • Predict meaning based on context, prior knowledge, and/or experience • Use context clues • Use linguistic knowledge • Identify the organizing principle of the text • Create inferences • Differentiate main ideas from supporting details in order to verify
Cultural Awareness	Uses own culture to derive meaning from texts that are heard, read, or viewed.	Generally relies heavily on knowledge of own culture with increasing knowledge of the target culture(s) to interpret texts that are heard, read, or viewed.	Uses knowledge of cultural differences between own culture and target culture(s) as well as increasing knowledge of the target culture(s) to interpret texts that are heard, read, or viewed.

ACTFL Performance Descriptors for Language Learners | **Presentational**

Domains	Novice Range	Intermediate Range	Advanced Range
	Communicates information on very familiar topics using a variety of words, phrases, and sentences that have been practiced and memorized.	**Communicates information and expresses own thoughts about familiar topics using sentences and series of sentences.**	**Communicates information and expresses self with detail and organization on familiar and some new concrete topics using paragraphs.**
Functions	Presents simple, basic information on very familiar topics by producing words, list, notes, and formulaic language using highly practiced language.	Expresses own thoughts and presents information and personal preferences on familiar topics by creating with language primarily in present time.	Produces narrations and descriptions in all major time frames on familiar and some unfamiliar topics.
	May show emerging evidence of the ability to express own thoughts and preferences.	May show emerging evidence of the ability to tell or retell a story and provide additional description.	May show emerging evidence of the ability to provide a well-supported argument, including detailed evidence in support of a point of view.
Contexts/ Content	Creates messages in some personally relevant contexts on topics that relate to basic biographical information.	Creates messages in contexts relevant to oneself and others, and one's immediate environment.	Creates messages fully and effectively in contexts both personal and general.
			Content areas include topics of personal and general interest (community, national, and international events) as well as work-related topics and areas of special competence.
	May show emerging evidence of the ability to create messages in highly practiced contexts related to oneself and immediate environment.	May show emerging evidence of the ability to create messages on general interest and work-related topics.	May show emerging evidence of the ability to create messages in more abstract content areas.
Text Type	Produces words and phrases and highly practiced sentences or formulaic questions.	Produces sentences, series of sentences, and some connected sentences.	Produces full paragraphs that are organized and detailed.

ACTFL Performance Descriptors for Language Learners | **Presentational**

	Novice Range	Intermediate Range	Advanced Range
Language Control	Produces memorized language that is appropriate to the context; limited language control may require a sympathetic audience to be understood. With practice, polish, or editing, may show emerging evidence of Intermediate-level language control.	Control of language is sufficient to be understood by audiences accustomed to language produced by language learners. With practice, polish, or editing, may show emerging evidence of Advanced-level language control.	Control of high-frequency structures is sufficient to be understood by audiences not accustomed to language of language learners. With practice, polish, or editing, shows evidence of Advanced-level control of grammar and syntax.
Vocabulary	Produces a number of high frequency words and formulaic expressions; able to use a limited variety of vocabulary on familiar topics.	Produces vocabulary on variety of everyday topics, topics of personal interest, and topics that have been studied.	Produces a broad range of vocabulary related to topics of personal, public, and community interest, and some specific vocabulary related to areas of study or expertise.
Communication Strategies	May use some or all of the following strategies to communicate, able to: • Rely on a practiced format • Use facial expressions and gestures • Repeat words • Resort to first language • Use graphic organizers to present information • Rely on multiple drafts and practice sessions with feedback • Support presentational speaking with visuals and notes • Support presentational writing with visuals or prompts	May use some or all of the following strategies to communicate and maintain audience interest, able to: • Show an increasing awareness of errors and able to self-correct or edit • Use phrases, imagery, or content • Simplify • Use known language to compensate for missing vocabulary • Use graphic organizer • Use reference resources as appropriate	May use some or all of the following strategies to communicate and maintain audience interest, able to: • Demonstrate conscious efforts at self-editing and correction • Elaborate and clarify • Provide examples, synonyms, or antonyms • Use cohesion, chronology and details to explain or narrate fully • Circumlocute
Cultural Awareness	May use some memorized culturally appropriate gestures, formulaic expressions, and basic writing conventions.	Uses some culturally appropriate vocabulary, expressions, and gestures. Reflects some knowledge of cultural differences related to written and spoken communication.	Uses cultural knowledge appropriate to the presentational context and increasingly reflective or authentic cultural practices and perspectives.